卞尺丹几乙し丹卞と

Translated Language Learning

The Nightingale and the Rose

夜莺与玫瑰

Oscar Wilde

English / 普通话

Copyright © 2023 Tranzlaty
All rights reserved.
ISBN: 978-1-83566-013-3
Original text by Oscar Wilde
The Nightingale and the Rose
Written in 1888 in English
www.tranzlaty.com

The Nightingale and the Rose
夜莺与玫瑰

'She said that she would dance with me if I brought her red roses'
"她说,如果我给她带上红玫瑰,她会和我一起跳舞"
'but in all my garden there is no red rose' cried the young Student
"可是我的花园里没有一朵红玫瑰,"年轻的学生喊道
from her nest in the holm-oak tree the nightingale heard him
夜莺从她在圣栎树上的巢穴里听到了他的声音
and she looked out through the leaves, and wondered
她透过树叶向外望去,心里想着

'No red rose in all my garden!' he cried
"我的花园里没有一朵红玫瑰!"他喊道
and his beautiful eyes filled with tears
他美丽的眼睛里充满了泪水
'On what little things does happiness depend!'
"幸福取决于哪些小事!"
'I have read all that the wise men have written'
"智者所写的,我都读过了"
'all the secrets of philosophy are mine'
"哲学的所有秘密都是我的"
'yet for want of a red rose my life is made wretched'
"然而,由于缺少一朵红玫瑰,我的生活变得悲惨"

'Here at last is a true lover,' said the nightingale
"终于有了一个真正的情人,"夜莺说
'Night after night have I sung of him, though I knew him not'
"我夜以继日地歌唱他,虽然我不认识他"

'Night after night have I told his story to the stars'
"我夜以继日地向星星讲述他的故事"
'and now I see him'
"现在我看到他了"

'His hair is as dark as the hyacinth-blossom'
"他的头发像风信子花一样黑"
'and his lips are as red as the rose of his desire'
"他的嘴唇像他欲望的玫瑰一样红"
'but passion has made his face like pale Ivory'
"但激情使他的脸像苍白的象牙"
'and sorrow has set her seal upon his brow'
"忧愁在他的额头上留下了印记"

'The Prince has organized a ball tomorrow,' said the young student
"王子明天组织了一场舞会,"年轻学生说
'and my love will be there'
"我的爱会在那里"
'If I bring her a red rose, she will dance with me'
"如果我给她带来一朵红玫瑰,她会和我一起跳舞"
'If I bring her a red rose, I will hold her in my arms'
"如果我给她带来一朵红玫瑰,我会把她抱在怀里"
'and she will lean her head upon my shoulder'
"她会把头靠在我的肩膀上"
'and her hand will be clasped in mine'
"她的手将紧握在我的手里"

'But there is no red rose in my garden'
"可是我的花园里没有红玫瑰"
'so I will sit lonely'
"所以我会孤独地坐着"
'and she will go past me'

"她会从我身边走过"
'She will have no heed of me'
"她不会理会我的"
'and my heart will break'
"我的心会碎"

'Here indeed is the true lover,' said the nightingale
"这确实是真正的情人，"夜莺说
'What I sing of he suffers'
"我所歌颂的，他受苦"
'what is joy to me is pain to him'
"对我来说快乐的，对他来说就是痛苦"
'Surely love is a wonderful thing'
"爱当然是一件美妙的事情"
'love is more precious than emeralds'
"爱情比祖母绿更珍贵"

'and love is dearer than fine opals'
"爱比精美的蛋白石更珍贵"
'Pearls and pomegranates cannot buy love'
"珍珠和石榴买不到爱情"
'nor is love sold in the market-place'
"爱情也不是在市场上出售的"
'love can not be bought from merchants'
"爱不能从商人那里买到"
'nor can love be weighed on a balance for gold'
"爱情也不能用天平来衡量黄金"

'The musicians will sit in their gallery,' said the young student
"音乐家们会坐在他们的画廊里，"这位年轻的学生说
'and they will play upon their stringed instruments'
"他们会用他们的弦乐器演奏"

'and my love will dance to the sound of the harp'
"我的爱人会随着竖琴的声音跳舞"
'and she will dance to the sound of the violin'
"她会随着小提琴的声音跳舞"
'She will dance so lightly her feet won't touch the floor'
"她会跳得很轻,她的脚不会碰到地板"

'and the courtiers will throng round her'
"朝臣们会围着她"
'but she will not dance with me'
"但她不会和我跳舞"
'because I have no red rose to give her'
"因为我没有红玫瑰可以送给她"
he flung himself down on the grass
他扑倒在草地上
and he buried his face in his hands and wept
他把脸埋在手里哭泣

'Why is he weeping?' asked a little Green Lizard
"他为什么哭泣?"一只小绿蜥蜴问道
while he ran past with his tail in the air
当他尾巴在空中跑过去时
'Why indeed?' said a Butterfly
"为什么呢?"一只蝴蝶说
while he was fluttering about after a sunbeam
当他在阳光下飘来飘去时
'Why indeed?' whispered a daisy to his neighbour in a soft, low voice
"为什么呢?"一朵雏菊用柔和而低沉的声音对他的邻居低声说

'He is weeping for a red rose,' said the nightingale
"他在为一朵红玫瑰而哭泣,"夜莺说

'For a red rose!?' they exclaimed
"为了一朵红玫瑰!"他们惊呼道
'how very ridiculous!'
"太荒谬了!"
and the little Lizard, who was something of a cynic, laughed outright
而那只有点愤世嫉俗的小蜥蜴,直接笑了起来

But the nightingale understood the secret of the student's sorrow
但夜莺明白了学生悲伤的秘密
and she sat silent in the oak-tree
她静静地坐在橡树上
and she thought about the mystery of love
她想到了爱情的奥秘
Suddenly she spread her brown wings
突然,她张开了棕色的翅膀
and she soared into the air
她翱翔在空中

She passed through the grove like a shadow
她像影子一样穿过小树林
and like a shadow she sailed across the garden
她像影子一样在花园里航行
In the centre of the garden was a beautiful rose-tree
花园的中央有一棵美丽的玫瑰树
and when she saw the rose-tree, she flew over to it
当她看到玫瑰树时,她飞到它身边
and she perched upon a twig
她栖息在一根树枝上

'Give me a red rose,' she cried
"给我一朵红玫瑰,"她喊道

'give me a red rose and I will sing you my sweetest song'
"给我一朵红玫瑰,我会给你唱我最甜蜜的歌"
But the Tree shook its head
但那棵树摇了摇头
'My roses are white,' the rose-tree answered
"我的玫瑰是白色的,"玫瑰树回答

'as white as the foam of the sea'
"像大海的泡沫一样白"
'and whiter than the snow upon the mountain'
"比山上的雪还白"
'But go to my brother who grows round the old sun-dial'
"但是去找我哥哥,他长在旧日晷周围"
'perhaps he will give you what you want'
"也许他会给你你想要的"

So the nightingale flew over to his brother
于是夜莺飞到他哥哥身边
the rose-tree growing round the old sun-dial
玫瑰树生长在古老的日晷周围
'Give me a red rose,' she cried
"给我一朵红玫瑰,"她喊道
'give me a red rose and I will sing you my sweetest song'
"给我一朵红玫瑰,我会给你唱我最甜蜜的歌"
But the rose-tree shook its head
但玫瑰树摇了摇头
'My roses are yellow,' the rose-tree answered
"我的玫瑰是黄色的,"玫瑰树回答

'as yellow as the hair of a mermaid'
"像美人鱼的头发一样黄"
'and yellower than the daffodil that blooms in the meadow'

"比草地上盛开的水仙花更黄"
'before the mower comes with his scythe'
"在割草机带着镰刀来之前"
'but go to my brother who grows beneath the student's window'
"但是去找我哥哥,他长在学生的窗户下面"
'and perhaps he will give you what you want'
"也许他会给你你想要的"

So the nightingale flew over to his brother
于是夜莺飞到他哥哥身边
the rose-tree growing beneath the student's window
学生窗下生长的玫瑰树
'give me a red rose,' she cried
"给我一朵红玫瑰,"她喊道
'give me a red rose and I will sing you my sweetest song'
"给我一朵红玫瑰,我会给你唱我最甜蜜的歌"
But the rose-tree shook its head
但玫瑰树摇了摇头

'My roses are red,' the rose-tree answered
"我的玫瑰是红色的,"玫瑰树回答
'as red as the feet of the dove'
"像鸽子的脚一样红"
'and redder than the great fans of coral'
"而且比珊瑚的忠实粉丝更红"
'the corals that sway in the ocean-cavern'
"在海洋洞穴中摇曳的珊瑚"

'But the winter has chilled my veins'
"但冬天让我的血管发冷"
'and the frost has nipped my buds'
"霜冻已经啃噬了我的花蕾"

'and the storm has broken my branches'
"暴风雨折断了我的树枝"
'and I shall have no roses at all this year'
"今年我就没有玫瑰了"

'One red rose is all I want,' cried the nightingale
"我只想要一朵红玫瑰,"夜莺喊道
'Is there no way by which I can get it?'
"难道我就没有办法得到它吗?"
'There is a way' answered the rose-tree'
"有办法,"玫瑰树回答说。
'but it is so terrible that I dare not tell you'
"可是太可怕了,我不敢告诉你"
'Tell it to me' said the nightingale
"告诉我,"夜莺说
'I am not afraid'
"我不怕"

'If you want a red rose,' said the rose-tree
"如果你想要一朵红玫瑰,"玫瑰树说
'if you want a red rose you must build the rose out of music'
"如果你想要一朵红玫瑰,你必须用音乐来建造玫瑰"
'while the moonlight shines upon you'
"当月光照在你身上时"
'and you must stain the rose with your own heart's blood'
"你必须用自己的心血染红玫瑰"

'You must sing to me with your breast against a thorn'
"你必须用胸膛抵着荆棘向我歌唱"
'All night long you must sing to me'
"你必须整夜唱歌给我听"

'the thorn must pierce your heart'
"荆棘必须刺穿你的心"
'your life-blood must flow into my veins'
"你的命脉必须流进我的血管"
'and your life-blood must become my own'
"你的命脉必须成为我自己的"

'Death is a high price to pay for a red rose,' cried the nightingale
"死亡是一朵红玫瑰所付出的高昂代价,"夜莺喊道
'life is very dear to all'
"生命对所有人来说都非常珍贵"
'It is pleasant to sit in the green wood'
"坐在绿色的树林里很愉快"
'it is nice to watch the sun in his chariot of gold'
"在他的黄金战车上看太阳真是太好了"
'and it is nice to watch the moon in her chariot of pearl'
"在她的珍珠战车上看月亮真是太好了"

'sweet is the scent of the hawthorn'
"山楂的香味是甜的"
'sweet are the bluebells that hide in the valley'
"隐藏在山谷中的风信子是甜蜜的"
'and sweet is the heather that blows on the hill'
"山上吹来的石楠花是甜的"
'Yet love is better than life'
"然而,爱胜过生命"

'and what is the heart of a bird compared to the heart of a man?'
"与人的心相比,鸟的心又算得了什么?"
So she spread her brown wings for flight
于是她张开棕色的翅膀准备飞翔

and she soared into the air
她翱翔在空中
She swept over the garden like a shadow
她像影子一样扫过花园
and like a shadow she sailed through the grove
她像影子一样在树林中航行

The young Student was still lying in the garden
那个年轻的学生还躺在花园里
and his tears were not yet dry in his beautiful eyes
他的眼泪在他美丽的眼睛里还没有干
'Be happy,' cried the nightingale
"快乐点,"夜莺喊道
'you shall have your red rose'
"你会得到你的红玫瑰"
'I will make your rose out of music'
"我会用音乐制作你的玫瑰"
'while the moonlight shines upon me'
"当月光照在我身上时"

'and I will stain your rose with my own heart's blood'
"我要用我自己的心血玷污你的玫瑰"
'All that I ask of you in return is that you will be a true lover'
"我只要求你做一个真正的爱人"
'because love is wiser than Philosophy, though she is wise'
"因为爱比哲学更聪明,尽管她是智慧的"
'and love is mightier than power, though he is mighty'
"爱比能力更强大,尽管他是强大的"

'flame-coloured are his wings'
"他的翅膀是火焰色的"

'and coloured like flame is his body'
"他的身体像火焰一样着色"
'His lips are as sweet as honey'
"他的嘴唇像蜂蜜一样甜美"
'and his breath is like frankincense'
"他的气息像乳香"

The Student looked up from the grass
学生从草地上抬起头来
and he listened to the nightingale
他听了夜莺的话
but he could not understand what she was saying
但他听不懂她在说什么
because he only knew what he had read in books
因为他只知道他在书本上读过什么
But the Oak-tree understood, and he felt sad
但橡树明白了,他感到难过

he was very fond of the little nightingale
他非常喜欢小夜莺
because she had built her nest in his branches
因为她在他的树枝上筑巢
'Sing one last song for me,' he whispered
"为我唱最后一首歌,"他低声说
'I shall feel very lonely when you are gone'
"当你离开时,我会感到非常孤独"
So the nightingale sang to the Oak-tree
于是夜莺对着橡树唱歌
and her voice was like water bubbling from a silver jar
她的声音就像从银罐里冒出的水

When she had finished her song the student got up
当她唱完歌后,学生站了起来

and he pulled out a note-book
他拿出一本笔记本
and he found a lead-pencil in his pocket
他在口袋里发现了一支铅笔
'She has form,' he said to himself
"她有形状,"他对自己说
'that she has form cannot be denied to her'
"她有形式,不能否认她"
'but does she have feeling?'
"但她有感觉吗?"
'I am afraid she has no feeling'
"恐怕她没有感觉"

'In fact, she is like most artists'
"事实上,她和大多数艺术家一样"
'she is all style, without any sincerity'
"她很有风格,没有任何诚意"
'She would not sacrifice herself for others'
"她不会为别人牺牲自己"
'She thinks merely of music'
"她只想着音乐"
'and everybody knows that the arts are selfish'
"每个人都知道艺术是自私的"

'Still, it must be admitted that she has some beautiful notes'
"不过,必须承认她有一些美丽的音符"
'it's a pity her song does not mean anything'
"可惜她的歌没有任何意义"
'and it's a pity her song is not useful'
"可惜她的歌没有用"
And he went into his room
然后他走进了自己的房间

and he lay down on his little pallet-bed
他躺在他的小托盘床上
and he began to think of his love until he fell asleep
他开始想起他的爱,直到他睡着了

And when the moon shone in the heavens the nightingale flew to the Rose-tree
当月亮照在天上时,夜莺飞到了玫瑰树上
and she set her breast against the thorn
她把胸膛靠在荆棘上
All night long she sang with her breast against the thorn
她整夜用胸膛靠着荆棘唱歌
and the cold crystal Moon leaned down and listened
冰冷的月亮俯下身子听着
All night long she sang
她整夜唱歌
and the thorn went deeper and deeper into her breast
荆棘越来越深地扎进她的胸膛
and her life-blood ebbed away from her
她的生命之血从她身上消失了

First she sang of the birth of love in the heart of a boy and a girl
首先,她唱出了爱在男孩和女孩心中的诞生
And on the topmost branch of the rose-tree there blossomed a marvellous rose
在玫瑰树的最顶端的树枝上,开着一朵奇妙的玫瑰
petal followed petal, as song followed song
花瓣跟着花瓣,歌跟着歌
At first the rose was still pale
起初,玫瑰还是苍白的

as pale as the mist that hangs over the river
像笼罩在河面上的薄雾一样苍白
as pale as the feet of the morning
像早晨的脚一样苍白
and as silver as the wings of dawn
像黎明的翅膀一样银光闪闪
As pale the shadow of a rose in a mirror of silver
苍白如玫瑰在银色的镜子里的影子
as pale as the shadow of a rose in a pool of water
苍白得像水池里玫瑰的影子

But the Tree cried to the nightingale;
但树向夜莺哭泣;
'Press closer, little nightingale, or the day will come before the rose is finished'
"再靠近一点，小夜莺，不然玫瑰还没开完，那一天就要来了"
So the nightingale pressed closer against the thorn
于是夜莺靠在荆棘上
and her song grew louder and louder
她的歌声越来越响亮
because she sang of the birth of passion in the soul of a man and a maid
因为她歌唱了一个男人和一个女仆灵魂中激情的诞生

And the leaves of the rose flushed a delicate pink
玫瑰的叶子泛起了淡淡的粉红色
like the flush in the face of the bridegroom when he kisses the lips of the bride
就像新郎亲吻新娘嘴唇时脸上的红晕
But the thorn had not yet reached her heart
但荆棘还没有到达她的心
so the rose's heart remained white

所以玫瑰的心仍然是白色的
because only a nightingale's blood can crimson the heart of a rose
因为只有夜莺的血才能染红玫瑰的心

And the Tree cried to the nightingale;
树向夜莺哭泣;
'Press closer, little nightingale, or the day will come before the rose is finished'
"再靠近一点,小夜莺,不然玫瑰还没开完,那一天就要来了"
So the nightingale pressed closer against the thorn
于是夜莺靠在荆棘上
and the thorn touched her heart
荆棘触动了她的心
and a fierce pang of pain shot through her
一阵剧烈的疼痛从她身上射出

Bitter, bitter was the pain
苦涩,苦涩是痛苦
and wilder and wilder grew her song
怀尔德越来越怀尔德的歌声
because she sang of the love that is perfected by death
因为她歌颂了因死亡而完美的爱
she sang of the love that does not die in life
她歌颂了生命中不死的爱
she sang of the love that does not die in the tomb
她歌颂了在坟墓里不死的爱
And the marvellous rose became crimson like the rose of the eastern sky
奇妙的玫瑰变成了深红色,就像东方天空的玫瑰
Crimson was the girdle of petals
绯红是花瓣的腰带

as crimson as a ruby was the heart
像红宝石一样深红色是心脏

But the nightingale's voice grew fainter
但夜莺的声音越来越微弱

and her little wings began to beat
她的小翅膀开始跳动

and a film came over her eyes
一层薄膜从她的眼前掠过

fainter and fainter grew her song
她的歌声越来越微弱

and she felt something choking her in her throat
她感觉到有什么东西扼住了她的喉咙

then she gave one last burst of music
然后她发出了最后一波音乐

the white Moon heard it, and she forgot the dawn
白月听见了,她忘记了黎明

and she lingered in the sky
她在天空中徘徊

The red rose heard it
红玫瑰听到了

and the rose trembled with ecstasy
玫瑰因狂喜而颤抖

and the rose opened its petals to the cold morning air
玫瑰向清晨寒冷的空气敞开花瓣

Echo carried it to her purple cavern in the hills
Echo把它带到了她在山上的紫色洞穴里

and it woke the sleeping shepherds from their dreams
它把沉睡的牧羊人从梦中唤醒

It floated through the reeds of the river
它漂浮在河边的芦苇丛中

and the rivers carried its message to the sea
河流将它的信息带到了大海

'Look, look!' cried the Tree
"瞧,瞧!"树喊道
'the rose is finished now'
"玫瑰花现在完成了"
but the nightingale made no answer
但夜莺没有回答
for she was lying dead in the long grass, with the thorn in her heart
因为她死在长长的草丛中,心里有刺

And at noon the student opened his window and looked out
中午时分,学生打开窗户向外望去
'What a wonderful piece of luck!' he cried
"真是太好了!"他喊道
'here is a red rose!'
"这是一朵红玫瑰!"
'I have never seen any rose like it'
"我从未见过这样的玫瑰"
'It is so beautiful that I am sure it has a long Latin name'
"它太美了,我敢肯定它有一个很长的拉丁名字"
he leaned down and plucked the rose
他俯下身子,摘下了玫瑰
then he ran up to the professor's house with the rose in his hand
然后他手里拿着玫瑰跑到教授家里

The professor's daughter was sitting in the doorway
教授的女儿坐在门口
she was winding blue silk on a reel

她把蓝色的丝绸缠绕在卷轴上
and her little dog was lying at her feet
她的小狗躺在她的脚边
'You said that you would dance with me if I brought you a red rose'
"你说过,如果我给你带来一朵红玫瑰,你会和我一起跳舞"
'Here is the reddest rose in all the world'
"这是世界上最红的玫瑰"
'You will wear it tonight, next your heart'
"你今晚会穿上它,紧挨着你的心"
'While we dance together it will tell you how I love you'
"当我们一起跳舞时,它会告诉你我有多爱你"

But the girl frowned
但女孩皱起了眉头
'I am afraid it will not go with my dress'
"恐怕它不会与我的裙子搭配"
'Anyway, the Chamberlain's nephew sent me some real jewels'
"不管怎么说,张伯伦的侄子送了我一些真正的珠宝"
'and everybody knows jewels cost more than flowers'
"每个人都知道珠宝比鲜花更贵"
'Well, you are very ungrateful!' said the Student angrily
"哎呀,你太忘恩负义了!"学生生气地说
and he threw the rose into the street
他把玫瑰扔到街上
and the rose fell into the gutter
玫瑰掉进了阴沟里
and a cart-wheel ran over the rose
一个车轮碾过玫瑰

'Ungrateful!' said the girl
"忘恩负义!"女孩说
'Let me tell you this; you are very rude'
"让我告诉你这个;你太粗鲁了'
'and who are you anyway? Only a Student!'
"你到底是谁？只是一个学生！
'You don't even have silver buckles on your shoes'
"你的鞋子上连银扣都没有"
'The Chamberlain's nephew has far nicer shoes'
"张伯伦的侄子有一双好看的鞋子"
and she got up from her chair and went into the house
她从椅子上站起来，进了屋

'What a silly thing Love is,' said the Student, while he walked away
"爱是多么愚蠢的事情，"学生说，他走开了
'love is not half as useful as Logic'
"爱不如逻辑有用"
'because it does not prove anything'
"因为它不能证明什么"
'Love always tells of things that won't happen'
"爱总是讲述不会发生的事情"
'and love makes you believe things that are not true'
"爱使你相信不真实的事情"
'In fact, love is quite unpractical'
"事实上，爱情是相当不切实际的"

'in this age being practical is everything'
"在这个时代，务实就是一切"
'I shall go back to Philosophy and I will study Metaphysics'
"我要回到哲学，我要学习形而上学"
So he returned to his room

于是他回到了自己的房间
and he pulled out a great dusty book
他拿出一本尘土飞扬的大书
and he began to read
他开始阅读

The End - 结束

www.ingramcontent.com/pod-product-compliance
Lightning Source LLC
Chambersburg PA
CBHW011955090526
44591CB00020B/2786